Berkshire

Berkshire

Nick Channer

Waterton Press Limited

First published in the United Kingdom in 1998 by
Frith Publishing an imprint of Waterton Press Limited.

British Library Cataloguing in Publication Data.

Nick Channer
Berkshire

ISBN 1-84125-045-7

Reproductions of all the photographs in this book are available as framed or mounted prints. For more information please contact The Francis Frith Collection at the address below quoting the title of this book and the page number and photograph number or title.

The Francis Frith Collection,
'Friths Barn', Teffont, Salisbury, Wiltshire, SP3 5QP
Tel: 01722 716376
E mail: bookprints@francisfrith.com
Web pages: www.francisfrith.com

Typeset in Bembo Semi Bold

Printed and bound in Great Britain by
WBC Limited, Bridgend, Glamorgan.

Contents

Francis Frith 1822–1898

Introduction
Francis Frith: A Victorian Pioneer

Francis Frith, the founder of the world famous photographic archive was a complex and multitudinous man. A devout Quaker and a highly successful and respected Victorian businessman he was also a flamboyant character.

By 1855 Frith had already established a wholesale grocery business in Liverpool and sold it for the astonishing sum of £200,000, equivalent of over £15,000,000 today. Now a multi-millionaire he was able to indulge in his irresistible desire to travel. As a child he had poured over books penned by early explorers, and his imagination had been stirred by family holidays to the sublime mountain regions of Wales and Scotland. "What a land of spirit-stirring and enriching scenes and places!" he had written. He was to return to these scenes of grandeur in later years to "recapture the thousands of vivid and tender memories", but with a very different purpose. Now in his thirties, and captivated by the new science of photography, Frith set out on a series of pioneering journeys to the Middle East, that occupied him from 1856 until 1860.

He took with him a specially-designed wicker carriage which acted as camera, dark-room and sleeping chamber. These far-flung journeys were full of intrigue and adventure. In his life story, written when he was sixty-three, Frith tells of being held captive by bandits, and fighting "an awful midnight battle to the very point of exhaustion and surrender with a deadly pack of hungry, wild dogs". He bargained for several weeks with a "mysterious priest" over a beautiful seven-volume illuminated Koran, which is now in the British Museum. Wearing full arab costume, Frith arrived at Akaba by camel seventy years before Lawrence of Arabia, where he encountered "desert princes and rival sheikhs, blazing with jewel-hilted swords".

During these extraordinary adventures he was assiduously exploring the desert regions of the Nile and recording the antiquities and people with his camera, Frith was the first photographer ever to travel beyond the sixth cataract. Africa, we must remember, was still the "Dark Continent", and Stanley and Livingstone's famous meeting was a decade into the future. The conditions for picture taking confound belief. He laboured for hours on end in his dark-room in the sweltering heat, while the volatile collodion chemicals fizzed dangerously in their trays. Often he was forced to work in tombs and caves where conditions were cooler.

Back in London he exhibited his photographs and was "rapturously cheered" by the Royal Society. His reputation as a photographer was made overnight. His photographs were issued in albums by James S. Virtue and William MacKenzie, and published simultaneously in London and New York. An eminent historian has likened their impact on the population of the time to that on our own generation of the first photographs taken on the surface of the moon.

Characteristically, Frith spotted the potential to create a new business as a specialist publisher of photographs. In 1860 he married Mary Ann Rosling and set out to photograph every city, town and village in Britain. For the next thirty years Frith travelled the country by train and by pony and trap, producing photographs that were keenly bought by the millions of Victorians who, because of the burgeoning rail network, were beginning to enjoy holidays and day trips to Britain's seaside resorts and beauty spots.

To meet the demand he gathered together a team of up to twelve photographers, and also published the work of independent artist-photographers of the reputation of Roger Fenton and Francis Bedford. Together with clerks and photographic printers he employed a substantial staff at his Reigate studios. To gain an understanding of the scale of Frith's business one only has to look at the catalogue issued by Frith & Co. in 1886. It runs to some 670 pages listing not only many thousands of views of the British Isles but also photographs of most major European countries, and China, Japan, the USA and Canada. By 1890 Frith had created the greatest specialist photographic publishing company in the world.

He died in 1898 at his villa in Cannes, his great project still growing. His sons, Eustace and Cyril, took over the task, and Frith & Co. continued in business for another seventy years, until by 1970 the archive contained over a third of a million pictures of 7,000 cities, towns and villages.

The photographic record he has left to us stands as a living monument to a remarkable and very special man.

Frith's dhow in Egypt c.1857

CHAPTER 1
WINDSOR, ETON & SURROUNDING VILLAGES

∽ DATCHET ∽

The scene of Falstaff's miseries in *The Merry Wives of Windsor,* Datchet stands on the Thames bank, opposite Home Park. One mile above the village, accompanied by the Provost of Eton College, the legendary angler Izaak Walton used to fish "for a little samlet or skegger trout, and catch 20 or 40 of them at a standing."

∽ ETON ∽

It was Henry VI who elected to mark the beginning of his reign in 1440 by founding a splendid church, attached to which would be a college of ten priests, four clerks, six choristers, and a school for 25 poor scholars. He chose Eton as his site - which at that time was a small, unknown settlement of little or no importance.

∽ HOLYPORT ∽

One of Holyport's most famous buildings is The Belgian Arms, which was originally the premises of a registered hatmaker, where coach passengers would call to buy a new hat or have their own brushed or cleaned. In its time, the inn has also been a fire station and a Wesleyan chapel.

∽ WINDSOR ∽

Much of Windsor is Victorian. The town is built on a hill overlooking the River Thames and dominated by its world-famous castle, the largest in England. The castle, which covers 13 acres, was chosen by William the Conqueror, though during his reign George IV spent nearly a million pounds on improving it.

∽ WRAYSBURY ∽

Once part of Berkshire, Wraysbury lies at one of the easternmost points of Berkshire. The thirteenth century church includes a Tudor pulpit and stands on the site of an archeological dig which yielded Mesolithic and Neolithic flints, as well as Saxon and Roman remains. Wraysbury was originally part of the Crown Lands of Windsor.

THE THAMES AT DATCHET, 1905. 53198

The riverside at Datchet has always been popular with visitors and locals, and the scene is enhanced by its views of Windsor Castle, Home Park and the Thames downstream which are particularly impressive.

THE GREEN AND MANOR HOTEL AT DATCHET, 1950. D9034

The Green, with its period buildings, lies at the heart of Datchet and this photograph, taken in 1950, captures an ice cream vendor waiting for business in the village centre. Before the M4 Motorway, traffic from London came through Datchet *en route* to Windsor.

DATCHET HIGH STREET, 1905. 53193

The railway at Datchet, pictured in 1905, runs between the Thames and the village centre. Datchet is mentioned in Shakespeare's *The Merry Wives of Windsor* and Jerome K. Jerome's *Three Men in a Boat*.

DATCHET, THE VILLAGE, 1905. 53194

A general view of the village, taken in 1905. Just before the turn of the century, Datchet suffered serious flooding when the swollen Thames caused a pond in the centre of the village to overflow. Several anxious residents were isolated in their homes.

ETON HIGH STREET, 1906.
With their top hats and stiff collars, Eton scholars, pictured in the High Street in 1906, have been an integral part of daily life in Eton since the College was founded by Henry VI in 1440.

56036A

THE COCKPIT, ETON, 1929. 81688
Eton boasts one of the most famous and picturesque streets in the country. This photograph, taken in 1929, shows the fifteenth century Cockpit restaurant which includes a knucklebone floor on which cock fights once took place.

COLLEGE BARNES POOL, ETON, 1914. 67007
The roof of Eton College Chapel, visible in this 1914 photograph, is a familiar sight in Eton. With the exception of the chapel, all the college buildings are built of brick - nearly two and a half million of them.

ETON, 4TH JUNE PROCESSION OF BOATS, 1906.   53724

This 1906 photograph captures the bustle and activity of one of Eton's most colourful events. On June 4th every year a procession of boats takes place to celebrate the birthday of George III, Eton's favourite monarch.

HOLYPORT, 1909.   61983

Several years after this photograph was taken in 1909, the East Berkshire village of Holyport became the setting for a First World War PoW camp and German soldiers were regularly seen marching through the village on daily exercise.

CLEWER, NEAR WINDSOR, 1890.   25618

This 1890 photograph shows the spire of St Andrew's church at Clewer, which is situated on the Thames, looking up towards Windsor Castle. Many servants of the royal household are buried in its churchyard.

WINDSOR BRIDGE, 1895.   35370

Photographed in 1895 and overlooked by Windsor Castle's famous Round Tower, Windsor Bridge was erected in 1822. Until the twentieth century, there was a toll - the living paid 2*d* while the departed could be carried across by coffin for 6/8*d*!

WINDSOR CASTLE LOWER WARD, 1895. 35380
This view, taken in 1895, shows the Lower Ward in the shadow of the Round Tower. Built against the south wall are the lodgings of the Military Knights, given their title by William IV in 1833.

QUEEN'S STATUE, WINDSOR CASTLE, 1895. 35380A
Gazing over the town of Windsor, the imposing figure of Queen Victoria, depicted here in 1895, two years before her Diamond Jubilee in 1897. It was Queen Victoria who famously decorated the Albert Memorial Chapel.

ST GEORGE'S CHAPEL, WINDSOR, 1895.   35387
Photographed in 1895, St George's Chapel is the resting place of kings – Henry VIII and Charles I are buried here. One of England's most impressive ecclesiastical buildings was begun by Edward IV in 1475 and completed during the reign of Henry VIII.

St George's Chapel, Castle Street, Windsor, 1895.   35394

Taken in 1895, this fascinating photograph shows the intricate detail and sumptuous carving of St George's Chapel. St George's is also the Garter Chapel and above the oak stalls of the Knights, hang their banners which remain there until death.

Riverside Gardens, Windsor, 1906.   53721

During the Victorian and Edwardian eras, the Thames riverbank drew large numbers of visitors who came here to enjoy the tranquil scene. Windsor's royal status made this stretch of the river especially popular, as witnessed in this 1906 photograph.

OLD TOWN HALL, WINDSOR, 1937.   88142

Photographed in 1937, the late seventeenth century Town Hall was designed by Sir Christopher Wren whose father was Dean of Windsor. This striking building includes an impressive baroque statue of Prince George of Denmark which was presented by Wren's son in 1713.

PEASCOD STREET, WINDSOR, 1937.   88141

Peascod Street, photographed in 1937, lies at the centre of Windsor, at the top of the hill. The town centre is characterised by its streets of essentially Victorian and Georgian buildings.

HENRY VIII GATE, WINDSOR, 1914. 66985
Windsor Castle's world famous entrance, photographed in 1914. By the sixteenth century, the main gateway was in such a poor state of repair that Henry VIII replaced it with one that bears his name.

ROMNEY LOCK, WINDSOR, 1906. 53722
Characterised by its granite steps, Romney Lock, photographed in 1906, lies on a reach of the Thames renowned for its close proximity to the playing fields of Eton. Windsor Castle's Round Tower can be seen against the skyline.

WRAYSBURY FERRY, 1890. 27246
This photograph shows the ferry at Wraysbury in 1890. The village was formerly known as Wyrardisbury, and in medieval times was part of the Crown Lands of Windsor. Magna Carta Island, where the famous charter was signed in 1215, is nearby.

Chapter 2
BRACKNELL, ASCOT & SOUTH EAST BERKSHIRE

ᕦ Ascot ᕤ

The village has grown and developed in the shadow of Ascot racecourse, which occupies an elevated position overlooking the surrounding area. Much of this corner of the county has fallen victim to the planner's axe, but pockets of open countryside and woodland still remain. Members of the Royal Family still drive through Windsor Great Park to attend race meetings at Ascot.

ᕦ Binfield ᕤ

Binfield, which lies just to the north of the rapidly expanding town of Bracknell, was once the home of Alexander Pope, the eighteenth century poet. Pope spent his childhood at Binfield and sang in the local choir. The construction of the fifteenth century church is unique to this part of the county: a striking mixture of Bagshot sand and ironstone.

ᕦ Bracknell ᕤ

Kelly's 1847 Directory described Bracknell as 'a small village 28 miles west of London. . . . being in a woodland county. . . .' Just over one hundred years later, in 1949, an official order designated an area of 1,860 acres in East Berkshire to become the site of Bracknell New Town, one of eight new towns built soon after World War Two to replace homes and industry destroyed in the London air raids.

ᕦ Crowthorne ᕤ

Crowthorne lies at the heart of a wooded landscape characterised by wellingtonias and rhododendron's, and dotted with red villas and more mellow houses. The towers and cupolas of Wellington College are glimpsed and nearby lies the formidable façade of Broadmoor Hospital, opened in 1863 and designed under the direction of Major General Sir Joshua Jebb.

ᕦ Sandhurst ᕤ

One of Sandhurst's most famous buildings is its church, which was completely rebuilt by Street in 1853 in sandstone, in an Early English style. Parts of the old village remain, though much of the town seen today developed as a result of the coming of the railway.

ᕦ Wokingham ᕤ

Wokingham has expanded enormously in recent years, influenced by its close proximity to London and the M4 Motorway. However, many of the market town's older buildings remain, and its charter was first granted by Queen Elizabeth in 1583. The restored parish church of All Saints includes a superb carved Perpendicular font.

ASCOT GRANDSTAND, 1901.   46866
Queen Anne established the famous racecourse in 1711, though the meetings only became popular when the Duke of Cumberland, the first member of the Royal Family elected to the Jockey Club, revived them later in the eighteenth century.

ASCOT GRANDSTAND, 1902   48276
After the death of his mother Queen Victoria, Edward VII did much to promote Ascot as a significant social event. This photograph of the racecourse was taken in 1902, a year after Edward became King.

ASCOT, 1906

55013

Ascot, close to the Surrey border and situated in a wooded corner of the county that was once part of the ancient Windsor Forest, has a strong suburban feel to it, with an abundance of Edwardian villas and shop fronts.

BINFIELD, THE STAG, 1892.

B97001

When this photograph was taken in 1892, Binfield was no more than a sleepy village. The Stag Inn dates back to the eighteenth century, and the elm tree on the right reputedly marked the centre of Windsor Forest.

HIGH STREET, BRACKNELL, 1961.
With New Town status and under the aegis of the Development Corporation, Bracknell began to expand rapidly. The town's first factory was in production by 1952 and by the time this photograph was taken in 1961, the population had quadrupled.

CHURCH ROAD, BRACKNELL, 1901.

46897

This photograph, taken in 1901, shows the shingled spire of Holy Trinity Church peeping above the rooftops in Church Road. Old Bracknell consisted of little more than a few houses and shops before New Town status allowed it to expand virtually beyond recognition.

HIGH STREET, BRACKNELL, 1901.

46893

More than 50 years before this photograph was taken in 1901, Bracknell was described in the county directory as 'a small village consisting of a long, narrow street, inhabited principally by small shopkeepers, who supply the surrounding neighbourhood.'

THE MARKET INN, BRACKNELL, 1951.   B172002
Bracknell, photographed here in 1951, grew up from the inns on the road between Ascot Heath and Reading, once a popular haunt of highwaymen who lay in waiting for their quarry among the trees of the old Windsor Forest.

HIGH STREET, BRACKNELL, 1901.   46894
A view of Bracknell's main thoroughfare in 1901. Some time during the second half of the nineteenth century, Bracknell became a town, helped by the coming of the railway in 1856 and the development of market gardening and brick-making.

HIGH STREET, BRACKNELL, 1901. 46895

Bracknell, seen here in 1901, was not considered the most prosperous of towns before the coming of the railway. Today, it is one of the largest industrial areas in the county.

CROWTHORNE HIGH STREET, 1921. 69934

The village of Crowthorne takes its name from a group of thorn trees at nearby Brookers Corner. At one time the name 'Albertonville' was suggested in honour of the Prince Consort. This view of the village high street was taken in 1921.

CROWTHORNE HIGH STREET, 1925.

Crowthorne grew and developed mainly as a result of two famous institutions - Wellington College and Broadmoor Hospital - both of which were built in the mid nineteenth century. This photograph, taken in 1925, shows the village high street.

CROWTHORNE, 1906.

Crowthorne has expanded in every direction since this photograph was taken in 1906. However, the influence of the Roman Occupation is still much in evidence. The Devil's Highway, a Roman road, passes through the village and two Roman milestones can still be seen locally.

LITTLE SANDHURST, 1939.
Sandhurst and Little Sandhurst in 1939. This part of East Berkshire consists almost entirely of nineteenth century development; here and there are a few large Victorian houses with huge plate-glass windows and free Renaissance decorations.

CROWTHORNE, 1925.   78035
By the time this photograph was taken in the mid-1920s, Crowthorne was firmly established as a community,
though the centre of the village really only dates back to the 1860s.

SANDHURST VILLAGE, 1906.   56999
Thirteen years before this photograph of Sandhurst was taken in 1906, the village police station was
completed in memory of some of Sandhurst's older residents. The building was later converted into flats, with
the bars removed from the cell windows.

SANDHURST, 1939. 88867
Sandhurst has expanded enormously in the second half of the twentieth century. When this photograph was taken, at the outbreak of the Second World War, it was a sleepy place in the shadow of the Royal Military College.

SANDHURST ROYAL MILITARY COLLEGE, 1911. 64049
The demand for peacetime army training led to the building of the Royal Military College early in the nineteenth century. This photograph of the Academy was taken in 1911, about one hundred years after it moved here from Berkshire.

SANDHURST ROYAL MILITARY COLLEGE, 1901.   46823
With its Doric edifice and handsome portico, the Royal Military College is one of Berkshire's most distinguished landmarks. This photograph, taken in 1901, captures the size and scale of the Academy.

MARKET SQUARE, WOKINGHAM, 1906.   57025A
Wokingham's triangular market place, photographed in 1906, is the town's focal point, dominated by its red brick Victorian town hall, which is triangular in shape and replaces a seventeenth century, timber-framed building.

CHAPTER 3

READING, TILEHURST & CAVERSHAM

⌒ CAVERSHAM ⌒

Caversham boasts a famous bridge spanning the Thames, first recorded as long ago as 1231. Henry III ordered the Keeper of Windsor Forest to 'deliver to Andrew, Sergeant of Caversham, one good oak to make a boat for ferrying poor people over the water of Caversham.' The cost of using the bridge was evidently too prohibitive.

⌒ THEALE ⌒

The village of Theale lies in the shadow of its unusually large Gothic Revival church, built between 1820 and 1832. In the heyday of coach travel, Theale wass a popular stop on the Bath Road, and the village High Street included many inns where passengers could enjoy 'cake and ale' while the horses were refreshed or changed.

⌒ TILEHURST ⌒

Reading's western suburb, Tilehurst takes its name from 'Tigel' meaning a wooded hill. Tiles were made in the village at one time, though the kilns have gone now, replaced by modern housing estates. Mostly, Tilehurst feels like a residential arm of Reading, which, essentially, is what it is, but here and there traces of the old village remain.

⌒ READING ⌒

Berkshire's county town is where Jane Austen went to school and Oscar Wilde was imprisoned. The town's industrial heritage is recorded in the local museum and the remains of Reading Abbey, founded in 1121 by King Henry Beauclerc, can still be seen. The Royal Berkshire Hospital, with its distinguished architecture, is also one of Reading's gems.

CAVERSHAM HIGH STREET, 1908.
During the Edwardian era, when this view was taken in 1908, Caversham was a popular address for affluent Reading residents. Much of the village lies on the north bank of the Thames, in the vicinity of the Henley road.

59968

THE RIVER THAMES AT CAVERSHAM, 1890.   27098

Photographed in 1890, the Thames can be seen meandering through Caversham, on the outskirts of Reading. There are only two bridges on this stretch of the river, which probably explains why Reading has not expanded on the north bank.

CAVERSHAM BRIDGE, 1904.   52027

Caversham Bridge, seen here in 1904, is one of Reading's most famous landmarks. The bridge played a key role in the Civil War with Charles I and Prince Rupert engaged in a fierce fight here against the Earl of Essex.

BRIDGE STREET, CAVERSHAM, 1908.

This photograph, taken in 1908, shows Bridge Street in the centre of Caversham, at the point where it crosses the Thames. The village became part of Berkshire in 1911, having previously been in neighbouring Oxfordshire.

ST PETER'S HILL, CAVERSHAM, 1908.

St Peter's Hill, photographed in 1908, climbs out of the village towards Caversham's striking parish church of St Peter, which occupies a pleasant setting above the Thames. The tower can be seen from the river, peeping through the trees.

Caversham from the Bridge, 1890.

A local resident described life in Caversham just before the turn of the century, when this photograph was taken, 'When we went shopping in the trap, we would stop outside the shop and the shopkeeper would come out and find out what we wanted.'

CAVERSHAM FROM CAVERSHAM HEIGHTS, 1908.
Caversham Heights, photographed in 1908, lies to the north of the Thames and began to expand up the valley slopes when Caversham became a fashionable suburb of Reading.

THE KENNET & AVON CANAL AT THEALE, *c*.1955.   T254008

Following the nationalisation of the railways in 1948, the Kennet and Avon Canal was closed to navigation in 1951, about four years before this photograph was taken in the mid-1950s.

TILEHURST, *c*.1960.   T48020A

The village of Tilehurst, photographed here in about 1960. The distinctive water tower, in Park Lane, constructed in 1931-2, is one of Tilehurst's most famous landmarks and can be seen from miles around.

SCHOOL ROAD, TILEHURST, *c*.1960.   T48027

Bustling School Road in Tilehurst, photographed in 1960, has long been lined with shops and houses. There used to be an old forge here, with a shed used for destroying unwanted horses and ponies.

ROEBUCK FERRY HOUSE, 1899.   43007

This photograph of Roebuck Ferry House, taken in 1899, is a reminder of the days when an un-accommodating landowner refused access to the Berkshire bank of the Thames. To facilitate horse-drawn barges and pedestrians, ferries had to transport them to the opposite bank.

THE THAMES AT READING, 1904.   52024

Reading is famous for the Huntley and Palmer biscuit works, once one of the town's biggest employers. For many years the Thames, photographed in 1904, played an important role in the success of the firm, carrying biscuits downstream to London docks.

SUTTON SEEDS, READING, 1912.   64639

Berkshire County Council's first Shire Hall, opened in 1911, a year before this photograph was taken in 1912. Adjacent to it are the stables (later the garage) of Suttons Seeds, once one of Reading's major employers, founded in 1806.

QUEEN VICTORIA STREET, READING, 1910.   62201

Reading is one of those towns that can only be appreciated on foot. A walking tour of its main streets and thoroughfares reveals much of architectural interest – particularly in the vicinity of Queen Victoria Street, photographed in 1910.

READING BRIDGE, 1924.   76255
Photographed in 1924, Reading Bridge is one of only two crossing points on this stretch of the River Thames.
To the east of it lies King's Meadow, and just beyond it, the confluence of the Thames and the River Kennet.

MARKET PLACE, READING, 1896.   37156
Reading's Market Place, pictured in 1896, survives more or less intact today. Overlooking it is the magnificent
fifteenth century tower of St Lawrence's church, founded in 1121. The south wall of the nave has a monument
to John Blagrave, a mathematician who died in 1611.

CAVERSHAM LOCK, READING, 1912.   64648
Until 1911, a year before this photograph was taken, Caversham had always been in Oxfordshire. The merging of the village into the borough of Reading was strongly resisted by the residents of Caversham.

MAIWAND MEMORIAL, READING, 1890.   27139
Forbury Gardens in Reading, photographed in 1890. The scene is dominated by a colossal cast iron lion weighing 16 tons, erected to commemorate 300 men of the Royal Berkshire Regiment who died in the Afghan campaigns of 1879-80.

BROAD STREET, READING, 1923.
During the early 1920s, when this photograph was taken, Broad Street was a busy part of Reading, bustling with cars, trams and shoppers. There were many shops, including drapers, hat shops, gents outfitters, shoe shops and a number of small cafes.

74436

PROSPECT PARK, READING, 1904.   52022
Two years before this photograph was taken in 1904, Reading Corporation was persuaded that Prospect Park should be bought 'for the benefit of weary workers who, when at rest, need some open space where communion with nature may be established...'

READING, 1924.   76256
The Thames at Reading, photographed in 1924, was often busy with steam barges, which regularly carried about 50 tons of imported grain from London to various mills, occasionally returning with beer from Reading's Simmonds Brewery.

MARKET PLACE, READING, 1870.   R13001
Buildings from several different periods overlook Reading's Market Place, photographed in 1870. At the centre of this picture is a distinctive stone lamp standard given by Edward Simeon in 1804 'as a mark of affection to his native town.'

ST MARY'S BUTTS, READING, 1912.   64641
St Mary's Butts, in the centre of Reading, photographed in 1912. The chequerboard flint and limestone tower of the Church of St Mary's is a distinctive local landmark. The church dates back to Saxon times.

KINGS ROAD, READING, 1924. 76243
This 1924 photograph shows Kings Road in Reading, at the point where it meets Cemetery Junction, to the east of the town. Reading's population expanded enormously during the nineteenth century and many new homes were built here.

CHAPTER 4

NEWBURY & WEST BERKSHIRE

⌘ HAMPSTEAD NORRIS ⌘

To the north of Newbury, on the edge of the downs, lies Hampstead Norreys, surrounded by hills and woodland. The church has an impressive flint tower, Norman doorways and a splendid Jacobean roof to the nave. The River Pang cuts through the village, as does the line of the former Didcot/Southampton railway, which closed in 1964.

⌘ HUNGERFORD ⌘

Famous for its many antique shops, which line the broad High Street, Hungerford was given a fishing charter and a brass drinking horn by John of Gaunt (the Duke of Lancaster), who granted fishing rights to the townsfolk. The Kennet, running through Hungerford, was once described as 'a fayre river which yieldeth store of fishes and especiallie trowtes.'

⌘ NEWBURY ⌘

The town is closely associated with two battles in the Civil War, the first in 1643, the second in 1644. The remains of Donnington Castle, once an important stronghold, can still be seen. Newbury's most famous inhabitant was surely John Winchcombe, better known as Jack O'Newbury, described as 'the richest clothier England ever beheld.' He began with nothing but ended up with over 200 looms.

CHURCH STREET, HAMPSTEAD NORREYS, 1950.   H149011

Cattle on the move through the village of Hampstead Norreys, photographed in 1950. During the Second World War, Folly Hill, which lies just outside the village, was the site of an airfield, with Wellington bombers based here.

HAMPSTEAD NORREYS PARISH WELL, 1959.   H149014

The Parish Well, photographed in 1959, was presented to the village by a resident of nearby Hawkridge in 1903. The well, no longer in use, stands beneath a tiled roof enclosed by wooden palings. The iron machinery for raising water is still intact.

HUNGERFORD HIGH STREET, 1903. 49383
This photograph of Hungerford High Street, taken in 1903, shows the ornately decorated Victorian town hall on the right of the picture. Many of the Georgian houses and shops are built in the red and blue brick so familiar to Berkshire.

HUNGERFORD HIGH STREET, 1903. 49384
Two hundred and thirty-five years before this photograph of Hungerford High Street was taken in 1903, Samuel Pepys visited the town and ate 'very good troutes, eels and crayfish' at The Bear Hotel. Twenty years later, in 1688, William of Orange accepted the throne of England here.

HUNGERFORD HIGH STREET, 1903.
Some of the original buildings in Hungerford High Street, seen here in 1903, were destroyed by several fires. Wide streets are typical of country towns, designed so that markets could be held without blocking the main thoroughfare.

BRIDGE STREET, HUNGERFORD, 1903   49386

This view, photographed in 1903, shows Bridge Street on the north bank of the Kennet and Avon. The canal and the railway brought prosperity to Hungerford, though the town's golden era began with the turnpiking of the Bath Road in the eighteenth century.

KENNET AND AVON CANAL, HUNGERFORD, *c.*1955.   H134005

This view of the Kennet and Avon Canal, taken in the mid-1950s from the Town Bridge, shows the site of Hungerford Wharf. J. Woolridge & Son, a local building firm, occupied the wharf for over 100 years before finally moving in 1962.

THE CLOCK TOWER, NEWBURY, 1952.   N61034

The clock tower, partly enclosed by an octagonal shelter and situated at the centre of a traffic system, stands on the site of a wayside chapel, disused in the sixteenth century, converted into houses and eventually demolished in 1791.

THE CLOCK TOWER, NEWBURY, *c.*1955.   N61039

This view of the Broadway was captured in the mid-1950s. The clock tower, originally distinguished by its exposed ironwork, has four illuminated dials and two drinking fountains and cost £278 and 5 shillings, subscribed by the townspeople.

TOWN BRIDGE OVER THE RIVER KENNET, NEWBURY, *c*.1955.

The bridge was built before the Kennet and Avon Canal, so there is no towpath. Access to Northbrook Street and the eastern side of the canal is *via* a narrow passage running beneath the buildings on the left of this photograph, taken in the mid-1950s.

VICTORIA PARK, NEWBURY, c.1955.

N61047

Victoria Park, to the east of Newbury town centre, photographed in 1955. Covering an area of seventeen acres, the park includes a statue of Queen Victoria, guarded by two terracotta lions which originally stood in the Market Place.

JACOBEAN CLOTH MUSEUM, c.1955. N61049

One of the town's most beautiful buildings, the Cloth Hall was restored in 1902, more than fifty years before this photograph was taken in the mid-1950s, in memory of Queen Victoria and handed to the Corporation who opened it as the Town Museum.

THE SWAN INN, NEWTOWN, NEAR NEWBURY, c.1955. N61052

The Swan, photographed in the mid-1950s, is characterised by its distinctive timber-framed façade. The inn, one of the most famous in the area, lies on the Berkshire/Hampshire border, just to the south of Newbury.

NEWBURY TOWN HALL, *c.*1965.

N61076

The Town Hall and its famous Clock Tower, photographed in the mid-1960s. This towering landmark, standing guard over the Market Place and seen from many parts of the town, was completed in 1881.

NORTHBROOK STREET, NEWBURY, *c.*1955.
On the right in this general view of Northbrook Street, photographed in about 1955, beyond Timothy Whites & Taylors, is the imposing façade of Camp Hopson department store, with its rubbed brickwork, Doric and Ionic pilasters, and tile-hung gables.

NORTHBROOK STREET, NEWBURY, *c.*1960.
One of Newbury's loveliest streets, depicted in about 1960, Northbrook Street is famous for its mid to late Georgian buildings, and distinctive pink and blue brick houses above lines of modern shop fronts.

THE WHARF, NEWBURY, *c.*1960.   N61105

At the height of the canal era, the Wharf was a bustling depot where up to ten large barges could load and unload. The long, galleried Granary, photographed around 1960, possibly dates back to the reign of Charles II and is now part of the Museum.

NORTHBROOK STREET, NEWBURY, *c.*1965.   N61111

Photographed about 1965, this view of Northbrook Street shows the façade of Newbury's famous department store, Camp Hopson, established in 1921. This part of the building is mid-Georgian with a moulded cornice and pediment.

BARTHOLOMEW STREET, NEWBURY, *c.*1965.   N61116

Bartholomew Street, on the southern side of the town centre, was originally called West Street. This general view, taken in about 1965, shows the street much as it is today - distinguished by its striking Georgian buildings.

NORTHBROOK STREET, NEWBURY, 1965.   N61124

Before the A34 ring road, through traffic passed along Northbrook Street - hard to imagine now! Some of the shops on the right of this photograph, taken in 1965, have Georgian fronts, while others date from the Queen Anne period.

NORTHBROOK STREET, NEWBURY, *c*.1965.
A general view of Northbrook Street, taken in the mid-1960s. The gable end to the left of the shop front, above which is a clock, is all that remains of cloth-maker John Smallwood's house.

N61130

THE TOWN BRIDGE, NEWBURY, 1956.   N61081

The present bridge, photographed in 1956, and noted for its stone dressings and balustrades, was completed in 1772 at a cost of more than £700 and replaces two wooden structures, one of which was destroyed by floods in 1726.

MARKET PLACE, NEWBURY, 1952.   N61024

This view of the Market Place, photographed in 1952, shows the old Beynon's department store. The shop was established in 1827 and originally lady customers were welcomed with a glass of wine, while the men were offered a glass of ale.

N61024

CHAPTER 5

BISHAM, MAIDENHEAD & SLOUGH

∽ BISHAM ∽

Situated between the River Thames and Quarry Woods, made famous in Kenneth Grahame's *The Wind in the Willows,* Bisham is one of Berkshire's most historic villages. Bisham Abbey was originally a preceptory of the Knights Templar and is mentioned in the Domesday Book. Queen Victoria is said to have called here whilst out driving in her carriage, but found no-one at home.

∽ MAIDENHEAD ∽

Maidenhead, an affluent Thames-side town, used to be a crucial stage post on the London to Bath road, and the nearby Maidenhead Thicket, an area of over 300 acres of woodland and peaceful glades, is well recorded as the haunt of highwaymen. Maidenhead's main street was once full of posting houses.

∽ SLOUGH ∽

It was John Betjeman who inadvertently helped to put Slough on the map with his famous lines: 'Come, friendly bombs, and fall on Slough, It isn't fit for humans now'. The town became part of Berkshire following the 1974 county boundary changes. Slough town centre is essentially modern, though a number of Victorian buildings survive.

BISHAM ABBEY AND CHURCH, 1890.
This photograph, taken in 1890, captures some gentle activity on the Thames, with tree-shrouded Bisham Abbey and church providing a splendid backdrop. Many water-colour artists have faithfully reproduced the serenity and timeless beauty of these surroundings over the years.

27237

BISHAM ABBEY, 1893. 31737

This splendid photograph, taken in 1893, shows Bisham Abbey overlooking a scenic stretch of the Thames. The rambling Tudor brick house stands on the site of an Augustinian monastery and fragments of the original abbey were used in its construction.

MAIDENHEAD BRIDGE AND RIVIERA HOTEL, 1893. 31751

Designed by Sir Robert Taylor, Maidenhead Bridge was rebuilt in 1777. This view of it was photographed in 1893. At the height of the coaching era, up to five hundred horses crossed the bridge daily.

MAIDENHEAD TURNPIKE, 1899.   43037

Maidenhead owes its importance to roads and transport. Long before the turnpike, photographed in 1899, the town may have been on the route of a Roman road, and a medieval bridge witnessed a good many fierce and bloody battles.

MAIDENHEAD HIGH STREET, 1911.   63797

A uniformed policeman on duty in Maidenhead High Street in 1911. Among the town's more famous shops was Biggs, a high-class jeweller, where Queen Mary frequently purchased gifts when staying at nearby Windsor Castle.

MAIDENHEAD HIGH STREET, 1890.   23634

How quiet Maidenhead High Street seems in this photograph taken in 1890, as the age of the motor car was just dawning. In later years the town became heavily congested with traffic when the Bath Road ran through here.

MAIDENHEAD HIGH STREET, 1921.   70909

At the height of the coaching era, Maidenhead was littered with posting inns either side of the High Street, seen here in 1921. Some of these hotels continued to thrive during the age of the motor car.

MAIDENHEAD HIGH STREET AND TOWN HALL, 1903.   50833

Typically, much of the older part of Maidenhead has long since disappeared, replaced by modern urban development. The original Town Hall in the High Street, seen here in 1903, was a solid, sturdy building squeezed between lines of shops.

KING STREET, MAIDENHEAD, 1904.   52372

With its close proximity to London and attractive riverside setting, Maidenhead became a fashionable resort in Victorian and Edwardian times, and was especially popular with wealthy Londoners, playboys and debutantes. This photograph of King Street was taken in 1904.

KING STREET AND CLOCK TOWER, MAIDENHEAD, 1911. 63801

The name Maidenhead means 'the maidens landing place' and this photograph, taken in 1911, depicts King Street and the town's splendid clock tower.

MAIDENHEAD BRIDGE, 1906. 54099

This photograph, taken in 1906, shows the graceful architecture of Maidenhead Bridge, distinguished by its elegant arches, striking stonework and fine balustrade. The original bridge was built in the thirteenth century.

BOULTERS LOCK, 1913.
A year before this photograph was taken in 1913, work was carried out to enable Boulters Lock to cope with the heavy pleasure traffic which reached its annual peak on Ascot Sunday.

65544

BOULTERS LOCK BRIDGE, 1906. 54082
During the Edwardian era, when this photograph was taken in 1906, Boulters Lock was a particularly fashionable spot on the river, with the scene brought to life by a colourful parade of punts and parasols.

BOULTERS LOCK, MAIDENHEAD, 1913. 65542

Fred Thacker waxes lyrical about Boulters Lock and its unspoilt setting in his *Thames Highway* -'a memory of Boulters Lock this which compensates for all the alien things of Maidenhead,' he says. This photograph was taken in 1913, a year after his visit.

BOULTERS LOCK BRIDGE, 1913. 77624

Boulters Lock is one of the River Thames' most famous landmarks, and during the Victorian and Edwardian periods drew large crowds of visitors in search of peaceful recreation. A boulter was another name for a miller.

BOULTERS LOCK, MAIDENHEAD, 1913. 65543

Boulters Lock, photographed in 1913, is probably the most famous lock on the Thames, and was the first and the lowest on the river of the first set of eight to be built under the legislation of 1770.

BOULTERS LOCK, MAIDENHEAD, 1906. 54083

This 1906 photograph captures the Edwardian gaiety of the Thames at Boulters Lock, a particularly fashionable spot with dozens of smart cruisers, punts and small craft parading before an admiring audience.

SLOUGH, 1950.   S256009

Slough, photographed in 1950, began to expand following Slough Estates' acquisition of 700 acres of derelict land in 1920. The company used the land to create a trading estate, something that at that time was considered enterprising and innovative.

SLOUGH HIGH STREET, 1961. S256031

Slough High Street, photographed in 1961. Many of Slough's town centre buildings are relatively new, dating from the post and pre- war periods. However, parts of the town are Victorian, which gives an extra dimension to Slough's character.

Slough High Street, 1950.   S256003

Slough dates back to the twelfth century when it was a hamlet on the London to Bath road. The settlement later spread to the neighbouring parish of Stoke Poges. This view of the High Street was taken in 1950.

WILLIAM STREET, SLOUGH, *c*.1955.   S256011

Long before this photograph was taken in the mid-1950s, Slough was an important staging post on the Bath Road. Daniel Defoe, who once journeyed this way, failed to understand how all the local inns could make a living.

CROWN CORNER, SLOUGH, *c.*1955.   S256010

According to Billing's directory of 1854, Slough, then a new town, already had a high street and, in terms of shops, was beginning to rival Eton, its older neighbour. This view of Crown Corner, Slough, was taken about one hundred years later in about 1955.

SLOUGH HIGH STREET, *c.*1955.   S256013

More than 10 years before this photograph was taken in the mid-1950s, a thick pall of oily black smokescreen enveloped the town and the trading estate, where many of the factories had been requisitioned for war work.

S256069

SLOUGH HIGH STREET, c.1965.
The success of the trading estate led to Slough, photographed in about 1965, being dubbed 'the hardest working town in Britain.' Many people moved here from the unemployment blackspots of South Wales and the North, swelling Slough's population to over 50,000.

Chapter 6
RIVER VILLAGES

∽ Cookham ∾

Cookham will forever be associated with the artist Stanley Spencer who died in 1959. Spencer was a controversial figure and even now, 40 years after his death, his work is the subject of speculation and debate. The village, which stands opposite Cliveden Woods, is also famous for a sarsen boulder known as the Tarry Stone, which has occupied different positions in the High Street over the years.

∽ Pangbourne ∾

Pangbourne is home to the famous Nautical College, established on top of a hill in the village in 1917. Prior to that, during the Edwardian era, Pangbourne became especially fashionable as a residential and holiday resort. D.H.Lawrence and his wife rented a cottage in the village in 1919.

∽ Sonning ∾

This beautiful Thames-side village was once a palace of the Bishops of Salisbury, having been part of the Church since the seventh century. The Deanery, one of Sonning's most famous buildings, was built for Edward Hudson, the owner of *Country Life,* in 1901, and designed by Sir Edwin Lutyens.

∽ Streatley ∾

One of Berkshire's prettiest and most famous villages, Streatley looks across the Thames to Goring, its Oxfordshire neighbour. The village occupies a truly outstanding position in what is known as the Goring Gap, where the river carved a new passage between the chalk hills during the last Ice Age.

∽ Wargrave ∾

The village is still remembered for the fire which all but destroyed the church on Whit Sunday 1914. The fire was probably the work of a militant wing of the Suffragettes - angry because the vicar would not withdraw the word 'obey' from the marriage service, though the claim was never proved.

∽ Bray ∾

Bray will probably always be known for its song "Whatsoever King shall reign, I will be the Vicar of Bray, Sir!" The village stands on a bend of the Thames, spanned at this point by a splendid redbrick bridge designed by Brunel. Seventeenth century gabled almshouses surround a quadrangle and the streets are lined with picturesque Georgian and timber-framed houses.

COOKHAM HIGH STREET, 1908.   61017

The controversial artist Stanley Spencer was born in Cookham in 1891, seventeen years before this photograph
was taken. The former Methodist chapel is now a gallery devoted to his work. Spencer used Cookham as the
background to many of his paintings.

COOKHAM, 1914.   67009

This photograph of Cookham was taken in 1914. In the early years of this century the village included an
apothecary, a butcher's shop - with traditional glazed tiles - a forge, dairy, a shoe-maker and an undertaker's.
Everything the residents needed could be acquired locally.

THE POUND, COOKHAM, 1914.   67013
The village of Cookham, seen here in 1914, is synonymous with the colourful tradition of swan-upping, which dates from time immemorial and involves the swans being upped, or counted, classified and marked. The Queen's swans are unmarked.

COOKHAM HIGH STREET, 1914.   67016
This 1914 photograph shows the seventeenth century Kings Arms Hotel, originally the Kings Head. A local woman once had her own special coinage for use only in the village, and a framed specimen of a half token still survives today.

ODNEY COMMON, 1925.
The Thames at Cookham used to have specifically designed woven baskets for catching eels, which were set up at various points along the river. This view of the Thames, taken in 1925, illustrates Cookham's potential for picnicking and relaxing by the water's edge.

77588

THE PANG, PANGBOURNE, 1890.   27072

The River Pang rises on the Berkshire Downs, beginning as an intermittent chalk 'winterbourne' before maturing to a clear trout stream. This photograph, taken in 1890, shows the river meandering past private gardens and farmland at Pangbourne.

THE PANG, PANGBOURNE, 1890.   27079

A classic view of the River Pang at Pangbourne, taken in 1890. The Pang is a typical chalk stream, swift and shallow and a perfect breeding ground for trout. Many varieties of plant grow in profusion along its banks.

Pangbourne Bridge, 1893.   31715

This view, photographed in 1893, shows the famous toll bridge linking Pangbourne with neighbouring Whitchurch, and still in private ownership today. The bridge, which spans the Thames, is famous locally for its distinctive cast iron lattice design.

PANGBOURNE VILLAGE, 1899.   42997

This view of Pangbourne shows the bridge over the River Pang, a tributary of the Thames. When this photograph was taken, at the turn of the century, the village was becoming a popular haunt of artists, writers and weekend anglers.

PANGBOURNE VILLAGE, 1910.   62218
Transport has always played a key role in the history of Pangbourne, photographed here in 1910. Its station on the Great Western Railway helped to widen its appeal as a popular inland resort. The ancient Ridgeway passes close to Pangbourne.

ROYAL OAK, WHITCHURCH, 1899.   43002
Whitchurch is Pangbourne's nearest neighbour and this 1899 photograph captures the atmosphere and feel of the village around the turn of the century. Sir John Soane, who rebuilt the Bank of England, was born here.

PANGBOURNE BRIDGE & GEORGE HOTEL, 1899.

A late nineteenth century advertisement for the George Hotel, photographed in 1899, reads: 'This house, being in the centre of the picturesque scenery of Pangbourne, affords every accommodation for tourists, boating parties or anglers visiting the neighbourhood. . . .'

42998

PANGBOURNE VILLAGE, 1910.   62217

This 1910 photograph shows W.H.Smith & Son on the left of the picture, a few yards from the road bridge crossing the River Pang in the centre of the village. W.H.Smith still occupies the same premises today.

PANGBOURNE WEIR, 1890.   27063

Some years before this photograph of Pangbourne Weir was taken in 1890, someone wrote of the village that it was 'another of those pearls of English landscape which our river threads; no sweeter is, within many miles.'

PANGBOURNE VILLAGE, 1910. 62220
This view of Pangbourne, was taken in 1910. On the left is the outline of the sixteenth century Cross Keys pub, one of Pangbourne's oldest buildings. Near it is Church Cottage, where Kenneth Grahame lived in the 1920s.

VIEW FROM THE SWAN AT PANGBOURNE, 1899. 43000
The view from the Swan Inn at Pangbourne, photographed in 1899. Kenneth Grahame, who wrote *The Wind in the Willows,* sought inspiration for his delightful story from this stretch of the river.

STREATLEY FROM GORING, 1896.
The village of Streatley, photographed from Goring in 1896, can be seen nestling between the Thames and the steep escarpment of the chalk downs, dotted with yews and junipers. The river is wide and shallow at this point.

SONNING VILLAGE, 1904.   52040

Sonning, pictured in 1904, includes many Georgian houses and timber-framed cottages. Dick Turpin supposedly galloped through the village on his horse, Black Bess, *en route* to his aunt's cottage after a hold-up on the Bath Road.

SONNING LOCK, 1890.   27159

The Thames falls gently by 4 ft at Sonning Lock, photographed in 1890. A short distance from here, the river is crossed by a bridge whose records indicate that it is the oldest on the Thames.

SONNING, 1917.   67959

Sonning, was once the home of Dick Turpin's aunt. The Thames is crossed by an ancient 200-year-old bridge and the lock here, photographed in 1917, regularly wins competitions for its dazzling flower garden.

STREATLEY FROM THE DOWNS, 1890.   27052

This photograph, taken in 1890, shows the village of Streatley on the left bank of the Thames. An old wooden bridge linked the village with Goring on the opposite bank until it was replaced in the 1920s.

STREATLEY VILLAGE, 1904.
This view of Streatley, photographed in 1906, shows the village centre. The Bull was once a coaching inn for the Royal Mail coach to Oxford. Early this century, much of Streatley was owned by the famous Morrell brewing family.

52933

WARGRAVE HIGH STREET, 1950. W25002

The village of Wargrave has an Edwardian feel to it, but its origins date back many centuries. The Bull, seen on the left in this 1950 photograph, was once a popular coaching inn, close to the busy Bath Road.

WARGRAVE VILLAGE, 1890. 27177

Many years before Wargrave grew in popularity as a riverside village, Edith, wife of Edward the Confessor, held the manor, and at that time it was known as 'Weregrave'. This photograph depicts Wargrave High Street in 1890.

BRAY LANDING PLACE, 1890.   23621

Four years after this photograph was taken in 1890, the Thames burst its banks and floodwater raged through Bray. According to local sources, a fish was even caught in the high street.

BRAY-ON-THAMES, 1929.
Famous for a ballad about its vicar, who, against a turbulent political climate, regularly changed his religion to avoid losing his very desirable living, Bray is one of the most attractive villages on the Thames. This photograph, taken in 1929, gives a flavour of its setting.

81693

BRAY VILLAGE, 1911. 63821

This photograph of Bray shows the village centre in 1911, with the perpendicular chalk and stone tower of the parish church of St Michael peeping above the rooftops. The church dates from Edward I and is built on the site of the original Norman church.

BROADMOOR ASYLUM ENTRANCE, 1908. 59488

This view shows the main entrance to Broadmoor Asylum, which is situated a few miles from Bray. Built on rising ground in 1863, Broadmoor is still in use today. It is one of four special hospitals providing treatment for psychiatric patients under secure conditions.

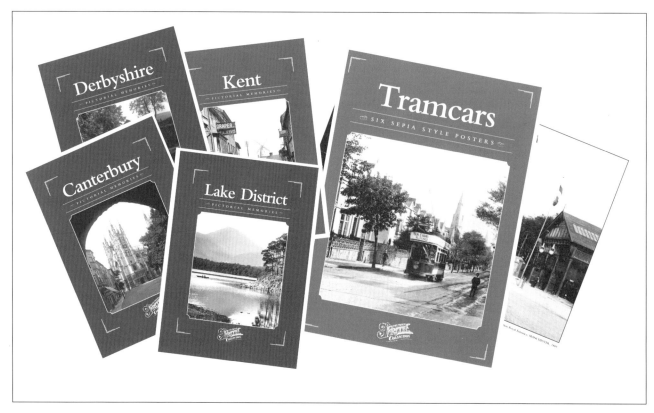

5   *Themed Poster Books*   £4.99

000-7	Canals and Waterways	
001-5	High Days and Holidays	
003-1	Lakes and Rivers	
004-x	Piers	
005-8	Railways	
044-9	Ships	
002-3	Stone Circles & Ancient Monuments	
007-4	Tramcars	

Town & City Series   £9.99

010-4	Brighton & Hove	
015-5	Canterbury	
012-0	Glasgow & Clydeside	
011-2	Manchester	
040-6	York	

Town & City series Poster Books   £5.99

018-x	Around Brighton	
023-6	Canterbury	
043-0	Derby	
020-1	Glasgow	
011-2	Manchester	
041-4	York	

County Series   £9.99

024-4	Derbyshire	
028-7	Kent	
029-5	Lake District	
031-7	Leicestershire	
026-0	London	
027-9	Norfolk	
030-9	Sussex	
025-2	Yorkshire	

County Series Poster Books   £4.99

032-5	Derbyshire	
036-8	Kent	
037-6	Lake District	
039-2	Leicestershire	
034-1	London	
035-x	Norfolk	
038-4	Sussex	
033-3	Yorkshire	

le *County Series*   £9.99

045-7	Berkshire	
053-8	Berkshire	
055-4	East Anglia	
077-5	Greater London	
051-1	Lancashire	
047-3	Staffordshire	
049-x	Warwickshire	
063-5	West Yorkshire	

County Series Poster Books   £4.99

046-5	Berkshire	
054-6	Berkshire	
056-2	East Anglia	
078-3	Greater London	
052-x	Lancashire	
048-1	Staffordshire	
050-3	Warwickshire	
064-3	West Yorkshire	

Country Series   £9.99

075-9	Ireland	
071-6	North Wales	
069-4	South Wales	
073-2	Scotland	

Country Series Poster Books   £4.99

076-7	Ireland	
072-4	North Wales	
070-8	South Wales	
074-0	Scotland	

A selection of our 1999 programme:
County Series and Poster Books
Devon, Cornwall, Essex,
Nottinghamshire, Cheshire.

Town and City Series and Poster Books
Bradford, Edinburgh, Liverpool, Nottingham,
Stamford, Bristol, Dublin,
Stratford-upon-Avon, Bath, Lincoln,
Cambridge, Oxford, Matlock, Norwich.

Themed Poster Books
Castles, Fishing, Cricket, Bridges, Cinemas,
The Military, Cars.

2007.

1337.
×5
___
52

4710